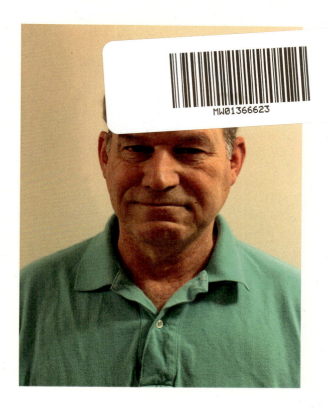

About the Author

Paul Devito got his master's degree in literature and has devoted his life to writing.

Of a Feather

Paul Devito

Of a Feather

Olympia Publishers
London

www.olympiapublishers.com
OLYMPIA PAPERBACK EDITION

Copyright © Paul Devito 2025

The right of Paul Devito to be identified as author of
this work has been asserted in accordance with sections 77 and 78 of
the Copyright, Designs and Patents Act 1988.

All Rights Reserved

No reproduction, copy or transmission of this publication
may be made without written permission.
No paragraph of this publication may be reproduced,
copied or transmitted save with the written permission of the publisher,
or in accordance with the provisions
of the Copyright Act 1956 (as amended).

Any person who commits any unauthorised act in relation to
this publication may be liable to criminal
prosecution and civil claims for damage.

A CIP catalogue record for this title is
available from the British Library.

ISBN: 978-1-83543-304-1

This is a work of fiction.
Names, characters, places and incidents originate from the writer's
imagination. Any resemblance to actual persons, living or dead, is
purely coincidental.

First Published in 2025

Olympia Publishers
Tallis House
2 Tallis Street
London
EC4Y 0AB

Printed in Great Britain

Dedication

I dedicate this book to Tami Rodriguez.

3/3/95

Out of the Storm

She flew in my window
with such a rush,
the wind swept back the curtains.
She looked at me and
alighted on the dresser
next to the vase of wildflowers.
She seemed so calm
all of a sudden, so happy
to be out of the storm.
I closed the window
and smoothed the curtains.
The candle finally settled down
and I sat down to eat dinner.
Suddenly, she lifted her wings
and flew around the room
quickly, around and around,
until she landed on my plate
and began to eat my bread.

3/8/95

Flight Around the Garden

Perched on the window sill,
my little bird looked out
at the trees and grass.
She wanted to be out,
to fly freely from branch to branch.
I opened the window
and moved the plant to the side.
The sun streaked the window pane.
She looked out and fluttered her wings,
jumped out and flew furiously
around and around the garden,
landing on the bird bath,
where she fluttered her wings,
splashing water on the flowers.
She watched me watching her,
shook the water off her wings
and flew back to my sill
to eat the sunflower seeds
I had scattered.

3/21/95

Broken Cage

One sunny day,
she flew in my window
and perched on my table.
I liked her so I put her in a cage
where she sat and couldn't fly.
We lived from day to day,
a little water, a little bread.
She seemed to like the cage all right,
until one day when I was cleaning it,
she flew around the room twice
and out the window,
ruffling the curtains as she went.
Now I sit by my window,
the cage broken in pieces,
waiting for my little bird to return.

3/30/95

Nesting

The light filtered lightly through
the window, she was sitting on the sill
waiting for the wind to stop blowing.
It was spring and she was building
her nest in the tree next to my house.
The wind gusted and the window
blew open, in she flew suddenly,
around and around the room,
looking for a place to settle.
Finally, she spotted my pipe
by my reading chair and swooped
down to dig some tobacco
from the bowl, then up again,
around in flight and out the window
again to her nest in the tree.

3/31/95

The Wind

Fluttering through blustering winds,
she beats her wings with fury
to arrive at my nest only a tree away.
Spring has arrived and the winds
have been furious the last few days.
She picks and claws at my twigs
in the nest to fill it up.
The colors of their feathers
lighter than mine, but her intensity
more serious, more meticulous.
The nest is everything. Paintings
hang on our walls like figures
from our past, our laughter
blending better with time.
She needs a strong bird,
one who flies great distances
at great heights, one who swoops
to great depths and arises again
stronger and stronger. Through the wind,
our nests one day will become one,
one day.

4/1/95

I Left My Window Open

Out the window she flies,
again, to scour the corners of the yard.
I lean out reaching for her,
but she slips away,
again, to search the corners of the yard.
Her wings are red today,
her brilliant colors attracting
all kinds of birds from far away.
She dodges and weaves,
flies high and low through the trees.
She wants to be chased
by the one she is chasing,
but the other birds can't keep up.
She flies so fast,
so quick to turn,
right through the wind,
her colors slowly turning
to blue and green
with dashes of yellow.
When she gets tired maybe she'll
fly back in my window.
Until then, I'll leave it open,
and at least let the sun in.

4/1/95

Secret Visit

My book rests open in my lap,
as I sleep in my chair,
the window slightly ajar,
letting the breeze gently in.
As I dream of far lights,
she enters the window and peeks around,
no movement but the music of Miles.
Plants and paintings everywhere
to amuse, she spots my pipe
resting by the book
and picks at the tobacco,
waking me up.
Startled, she flies around the room,
fluttering her wings furiously.
There seems to be no way out,
until I gently open the window.
Out she goes to the tree in the yard,
my laughter frightening her away.

4/2/95

Wind Song

A bitter cold gust of wind
pushed the window wide open.
Out she went as if the outdoors
had called for the first time.
She flew high above the trees,
wings outstretched, riding the wind,
then down again, through the yard
with such speed she was gone in a
flash.
Around the town.
in search of more room to fly,
then just as quickly she returned
and rested on my sill.
I was reading by the light
and watched her watch me,
neither of us moved,
until I got up and opened her cage.
New straw, food and water.
She looked twice, whistled,
then flew back in her cage
with a brilliant burst of singing.

4/4/95

Furthest Tree in the Yard

She raged in fury
against her cage as I put
a little water in her bowl.
She picked at the water
and flicked it at me.
There was no appeasing her,
her laughter had disappeared.
I opened the cage
and watched her watch me
in disbelief. She hesitated
momentarily, then lifted her wings
and out she went,
fluttering her wings furiously
around the room.
I opened the window,
and out she went
to the furthest tree in the yard.
Now it's been a few days
and she hardly moves from the tree.
I sit waiting, hoping
somehow she'll think she's
better off in my cage.

4/6/95

Brief Visit

She has little laughter,
with her mother's death died
the secret child smile within her.
Still, she flies high,
surveys all the land,
can catch any other bird
with one fell swoop.
I saw her fly by my window
one day, pretty colors,
nice feathers, sharp eyes,
her flight of a different pattern,
never seen before or since,
with motions beyond beauty,
circles and lines
only a poet could follow.
I left my window open the other day,
and in she flew with bright eyes.
She pecked at my tobacco
and flew out again just as quickly.

4/8/95

Scratching at My Pipe

In she flew again,
with the lightness of light,
alighting on the sill
to watch me read and smoke.
She flew around the room twice,
once to survey and once to show off,
her yellow blue feathers outstretched,
her eyes focused on my tobacco.
As I pretended to sleep
with my book wide open,
she tiptoed over to my pipe
and scratched at some tobacco.
It was the only thing she needed.
She flew back to the sill,
tipped her head as if in thanks,
and flew furiously to her nest
she was building in the tallest
tree in the backyard.

4/13/95

Always in Flight

She wouldn't sing in her cage,
so I let her out to fly
about the room. Evening light
filtered through the window,
her wings of gold and blue
flapped furiously as she
tried to find a way outside.
She was getting tired of flying
in circles. I wanted to put her
back in her cage, but the wind
suddenly pushed open the window,
and out she went to the maple
in my backyard. I put sunflower
seeds in my feeder to lure her
closer to my window, but she
kept her distance, kept her song
to herself and watched me closely
as I climbed the tree
to try to catch her. She waited
till I got to the top
and flew back to my window
to eat the seeds,
back and forth.

Always in Flight - Continued

we played our game, from nest to nest,
until I gave up in frustration.
I fell asleep reading my book.
She pushed open the window
and began to sing.
I awakened from my dream
just in time to see her fly away.
Now I was forced to wait,
perhaps in vain, for her to return.

4/14/95

From Yard to Yard

She has flown away
again. I left the window open
by mistake. I was hoping
she would stay in the backyard
in the oak or maple,
rustling leaves felt like they
were waving goodbye to her.
I have a feeling I know
where she went, another yard
not too far away,
where she tastes the fruits
she can't get from me—
apple trees and cherries.
I'll wait patiently with the oak
next to my house,
my window open, Miles
playing in the background.
She'll be back, I know it.

4/16/95

A Gift from Myself

I hadn't seen her for days,
a fresh rain had cleaned
the birdbath in the backyard.
Early this morning, I was looking out
and saw her quietly alight
on the basin, she fluttered her wings,
splashing water into a mist
that washed her body's feathers.
She seemed glad to be back
from such a long flight perhaps.
After her bath she flew to my window
and peeked in, just as I was
taking my bath, she flew over
to my tobacco pouch and took out
a little, I thought then that she was
headed for her nest in the great oak
out back, but instead she flew
around the room twice, and put
the tidbit of tobacco in my pipe
that was resting by my chair.
A gift, I thought, and out she flew
again with a high pitched song.

4/16/95

Bird Catcher

Suddenly a shot rang out.
I quickly looked out the window
to see her dodging through the trees,
but I went to stop the shooting,
to find a little boy with his father's
gun, pointing in every direction,
taking potshots at my little one
flying around, I took the gun
and pointed to my little bird,
"watch her now."
She flew around up and down,
and swooped to splash
in the birdbath. The sun was shining
down into my garden; the flowers
were breathtaking this spring.
She took her bath slowly, splashing
everywhere, bringing other birds
to her side. The boy was so delighted,
he took the gun and broke
it over a rock.

4/18/95

The Great Return

She flew such a long distance,
I thought she might not return,
but on Sunday, early in the morning,
I heard her distinct song.
She had left her eggs in the nest,
and now she was at my window.
I opened it and let her in.
She flew around the cage
that she used to live in,
and around the room,
she flew with such vigor,
then suddenly she alighted on my book,
to rest and watch me.
Her feathers bright blue,
a gift in her beak I noticed.
She placed it on my book
and flew back to the window,
then out with a rush.
I was so curious I looked
and could not believe my eyes,
a bit of tobacco from far away.

4/21/95

Rainbow

She was out in the garden,
sunning herself by the roses.
Suddenly, a rain cloud stopped by
and a gentle sunrain began to fall.
She flew up to her nest in the oak
and protected her babies.
The sun was stretching in various
directions and a rainbow was formed
in the west. The other birds
hardly noticed the rain; they played
in the birdbath, splashing merrily
as if time stood still.
Then the cloud passed. My bird
flew down from her nest
and joined the others in the bath.
The flowers glistened with the drops
of water as if dew had fallen.
No catastrophe had occurred,
nothing at all hardly but a few drops
of water, and yet everything was different.

4/22/95

Long Flight Home

She was tired from the long flight,
but she came to my window
without a moment's hesitation.
Her feathers were so bright,
I let her in to rest upon
my chair, she started singing
and flying about the room
with a second wind.
She was so glad to be home.
I lit my pipe and started to smoke,
something that always delighted her.
I watched her watch me
and sing the most beautiful song
I had ever heard.
Those long trips were painful
for both of us,
but the reunions made them all worthwhile.

4/22/95

Flight of the Crow

She was by the roses this morning
enjoying the early sun,
when she saw a crow flying
toward her nest. The crow's laughter
was deafening, had lost its balance,
like a lover had died,
and now was taking revenge
on my beautiful cardinal.
She swiftly flew up through
the pines to her nest in the oak.
Her eggs were safe and she quickly
chased off the sickly crow
who had nothing better to do.
I smiled at her as she returned
to the birdbath and showed her
my gun in case he returned.

4/23/95

Morning Visit

A new bird flew into my garden
early this morning, dark beautiful
colors, with a free high pitched song.
She was visiting my birdbath
and somewhat frightened the other birds
away for a while, until she showed
she was friendly and not trying
to keep the birdbath all to herself.
The others warmed up to her
after a while and my cardinal
welcomed her with a chipper song.
They played and played
until my bird came to my window.
I opened it and put some birdfeed
on the sill, she ate and waited
for the new dark bird to join her.
Sure enough the new bird came
to feed at my window and the
two of them kept me company
all morning, we had a new friend,
and there was room in the garden
for all of us.

4/25/95

Light and Shadow

She swooped and dipped,
rolled over in the air,
and flew straight up above the trees,
then down again to the birdbath.
She was celebrating the morning
since a male cardinal had entered
the garden. The dew glistened on the petals
of the spring flowers, reds and whites
highlighted the greens and browns
of the garden. She was showing off,
the moment was hers, the light
of the sun could barely keep up,
in the mating dance of light
and shadow. Then she settled
down and came to feed at my window.
I opened it and let her in.
She immediately went over to my tobacco
pouch and took out a little,
then out the window again
to show her new friend what
she had brought for the nest.

4/26/95

Light's Reflection

Her song sounded like laughter,
as she flew gracefully around the garden,
from flower to flower branch to branch,
as though this were the last moment
of sunshine. Then she alighted
on the birdbath, the water
glistening on her fluttering wings.
A male cardinal watched her
from a distance, his eyes feasting
on the most beautiful bird of all.
I left my window open
as I sat on my chair and smoked
my pipe, I put birdseed on the sill,
I waited patiently but she
never came to the window.
I would have to watch her
from a distance, knowing sooner
or later she would return
to my window.

4/28/95

Early Bird

A yellow bird has entered our garden,
of sharp plumage and intricate flight.
She came to my window this morning
to eat a lot of seed, her eyes
bright blue, her feathers all puffy
with beauty, a canary from local
haunts, with a bright lonely song.
The spice has gone out of her flight,
but our garden is beautiful,
colorful flowers in reds and blues
dressed by the greens of the foliage.
She seemed to have a question for me,
she had been watching my cardinal
all morning to find her patterns.
Her question was simple and I
Accepted. She came in the window
to fly around the room furiously,
then gently alighted by my book
resting on my chair. She took a little
tobacco out of my pipe and flew
quickly out the window, to the maple
in the garden, she began to build
her nest in the finest garden of all.

4/29/95

Caged

I heard a tapping on my window
in the middle of the night.
My canary was still awake,
she wanted to come in and sit
by my book. She seemed frightened
from the blustering winds of the night.
I turned on my lamp by the chair,
and sat quietly with my pipe
in my mouth. She spoke in soft
tones of problems she was having,
chirping busily about this and that.
I put my hand on her
and put her in my cage.
She started to sing,
and even though I left the door
open, she wouldn't leave.

5/1/95

Sudden Flight

She flew away one morning,
without notice, to a garden far away.
A bird of paradise attracted her,
with red and blue feathers,
without the laughter
that had kept her in my garden.
I looked out the window
early in the morning
to find her gone.
What a terrible feeling.
I sat in my chair and smoked
my pipe, there was nothing
to do but wait.
I didn't know if she would return,
she left her nest undisturbed.
I feared this day might come.
The hours dragged by,
until late in the evening,
she returned, all tired out.
I left the window open,
but she stayed in her nest.
perhaps I would see her in the morning.

5/1/95

Night Flight

Flying high at night
through the trees,
she spreads her wings
with the majesty of a condor.
She is free to fly where she will,
our garden bathes in the moonlight.
I see her like a shadow
gliding through the evening breeze.
She likes the night,
her flight is freer
turned away from the droll patterns
of the day. Her song
deeper and lighter at the same time.
In the middle of the night
she discovers herself,
can find a bit of laughter
in the shades of fine light.
She feels life will be longer
if she flies at night.

5/3/95

Up Up and Away

She's been gone for three days,
the garden rests quietly
in the morning light.
The other birds are not as playful
when she's away.
I had closed my window
the other day for the first time.
I was angry at her
for flying away so often.
Now I don't know if she'll return,
the backyard is too quiet,
even the flowers seem duller.
The breeze won't budge the leaves
that are so willing to dance.
The silence is maddening.
I open my window
and put a little seed on the sill.
Now I sit, unable to read,
unable to smoke, waiting for my bird,
who may never return.

5/3/95

Back Again

She returned in the morning,
after days of being away.
Her feathers were ruffled and worn
from the long flight.
she was tired and went right to her nest.
I was so overjoyed
I hid from my open window.
I sat comfortably in my chair
and lit my pipe.
She had learned something,
perhaps it was painful.
A couple of hours later she flew
down to the birdbath
to bask in the golden sun.
The water soothed her muscles.
She felt at home,
and even though she avoided
my window for a day,
I knew she was back for a while.

5/4/95

Bathing Beauty

Her flight was peculiar
this morning, dives and swoops
as though she were happier
than usual. The nest was waiting
for a male bird, and she
was showing off for the birds
in the neighborhood. Her feathers
were bright in the morning light.
She flew from branch to branch,
hopping from garden to garden
with a mere gesture of her wings.
then as she tired,
she decided to bathe herself
in my birdbath. She never
bathed anywhere else. The others
would have to be brave
enough to enter her garden
in order to bathe with her.
Few dared the move.
Now she was bathing alone
while we all watched.

5/5/95

Climbing

I climbed up the tree,
first thing in the morning,
to look inside her nest.
She had laid eggs days before,
and now I wanted to see how
they were doing. The garden was alive
with sunlight, petals quivered
in the gusty breeze.
The climb was arduous, but in a few
minutes I was peering into her nest.
The three eggs lay quietly
and unharmed in the robust nest.
She stood on a branch nearby
watching me closely, knowing
what I was doing, enjoying my
movements as I climbed back down.
She came to visit me at my window,
listened to me play the piano,
and let the time pass,
ever so slowly.

5/9/95

Trappings

Away she flew
one day, without notice
for seven days. She left a yellow
feather in her nest, a reminder
of her grace in flight.
This morning she returned
with a smile on her face.
She was playing with me,
flying away for days
then coming back,
as if nothing had happened.
She came to my window
and nudged it open.
She had brought me some tobacco
from far away,
as if she'd made the trip for me,
testing, always trying her freedom.
One day I'll close the window
behind her and keep
her song for myself.

5/16/95

The Storm

A storm hit the garden
this morning. The flowers
were thrown from side to side
and pelted with heavy drops.
The birds were hiding
in the trees, as they waved
in the strong winds.
An orange bird
had recently entered our garden,
as troubled as the storm,
her feathers bright with color,
her wings strong and able.
She stayed away from the other birds,
she hung by my window
waiting for me to open it.
When the storm hit, I let her in
to fly about my room.
She seemed so happy
she began to sing.
I would have to wait patiently
for the storm inside and out,
to subside.

5/17/95

Weary Return

I was sound asleep in my chair,
the blustering wind blew open
my window. She struggled in
with torn feathers and bruised body,
she had been gone for two days.
The light by my chair
cast a weak light across the room.
She seemed dejected,
the flight had been very long.
Now she was coming to me
late in the evening
to explain her leaving,
"I didn't want to leave, you made me!"
I had no answer for her.
I offered her some birdseed
which she gladly accepted.
I sat quietly in my chair,
watching her, knowing I could
do nothing to change her mind.
Just as I was about to speak,
she flew out the window
to her nest in the great oak.

5/28/95

Short Fall

Out of the air she fell,
as if her wing had been clipped.
She fell in the flowers,
by the birdbath.
I picked her up
and brought her inside.
I sat in my chair
and lit my pipe
as I tended to her.
Her eyes were tired and sad,
she was not physically hurt,
just very tired,
too weary to go on.
I gave her some water
and some birdseed.
In an hour she perked up,
regained her strength,
and flew out the window,
back to her nest in the oak.

6/17/95

Morning Crisis

The garden was peaceful at dawn,
the dark blue sky was slowly
turning orange and pink.
My cardinal was singing merrily,
leading the chorus in my trees.
I opened my window
and let the summer breeze in.
I spread birdseed on the sill
and waited patiently for them to come.
I lit my pipe and made coffee,
it was going to be a perfect day.
I watched the wispy clouds
change colors as the sun
rose slowly and quietly.
Suddenly, a squirrel charged
up the oak and invaded
my cardinal's nest, looking
for trouble and finding it.
All the birds gathered around
and began attacking the squirrel.
It wasn't long before his retreat.
The danger had passed,
in a few minutes tranquility
returned and the birds began
to sing in unison.

6/19/95

Flight from the Garden

The garden lay calm in the sweltering heat.
June had taken a turn toward August,
the birds were singing,
but feeling the intense heat.
I filled the birdbath with cool water.
And watched them gather like a party.
They splashed and sang,
fluttered and flittered in the water.
I watered the flowers
and sat in the shade of the maple.
Time moved slowly.
My cardinal seemed restless,
as the others played in the bath.
She flew up and around,
dove down, swooped and dipped,
as if the garden couldn't contain her.
Suddenly, she flew away,
perhaps to a distant garden.
The others grew quiet
as they watched the red feathers
disappear in the distance.
Now the heat was overwhelming,
another waiting had begun.

6/20/95

Morning Shower

I heard them singing before dawn,
always chipper no matter the weather.
I got up even though feeling tired,
made coffee and lit my pipe.
Dark clouds hung over the horizon,
thunderstorms lurked as the heat
began to rise. The birds fluttered
around the birdbath enjoying
the morning as usual. I spread
some birdseed on the sill,
and put some jazz on the stereo.
I had to shoo away the squirrels
from the birdseed, waiting
patiently for the birds to visit.
Suddenly, a clap of thunder
boomed from the sky,
lightning flashed through the garden.
The birds grew quiet
and flew into the trees.
Rain began to pour through
the stifling heat. We needed
the rain, there would be no playing
today. My garden came back to life.

6/21/95

The Great Outdoors

I always kept her in the cage,
fed her water and birdseed every morning.
She sang to her heart's content,
then one morning I let her out.
She flew about the room twice
and settled next to my chair.
I lit my pipe and sat with her,
reading and listening to jazz.
She seemed so content,
then she flew to my window
and looked out at the other birds.
She stopped singing and just watched,
they were playing in the birdbath,
fluttering their wings offbeat.
Suddenly, she looked so sad,
I wanted to put her back in the cage
but she flew around the room furiously.
There was no containing her.
I feared she would fly from the garden
if I opened the window,
but I took a chance
and let her fly outside.
She went to the birdbath
and played with the others.
She began to sing again,
so I closed the window and began to cry.

6/22/95

I Closed My Window

Out she flew,
for the last time.
I could tell she wouldn't be back,
her nest had been destroyed.
Even the flowers in the garden
looked wilted.
Now a steady rain,
after a dry spring,
I closed the window
and sat in my chair,
lit my pipe and listened
to Miles playing like a bird.
It was finally over.
The others gathered around
the birdbath to mourn
the loss, I almost felt relieved,
I couldn't take
the flights to the other gardens.
I couldn't wait anymore,
now she was gone.

6/23/95

I Wish I Could Fly

It was still dark out when I awakened,
the birds weren't yet singing.
I was startled out of a bad dream;
they had all flown away,
leaving the garden bare.
I couldn't get back to sleep,
so I made coffee and lit my pipe,
turned on the light next to my chair,
and began to read.
As the sky turned light blue,
I heard my cardinal leading the chorus;
they were still here,
I was so grateful.
I opened my window and put seed
on the sill, they came to feed
singing the most cheerful song.
As the sun rose in the sky,
they flew to and fro, up and down,
the flowers waved in the breeze.
How I wanted to live with them,
sing with them and fly,
soar high above the world,
give up everything for the feeling
of flight, in a garden of so many
flowers, so much freedom.

6/25/95
Stranger in the Garden

It was late in the evening,
the birds were tired and quiet,
the orange sun hung on the horizon.
Suddenly, a strange bird
flew into our garden,
obviously from very far away.
Her colors were perfectly unique;
never had I seen a bird like her.
The others stared and gawked,
watched her invade their birdbath.
At first, they seemed jealous
and wouldn't play with her,
then they grew to like her,
and joined her at the bath.
She instantly became the leader,
even my cardinal followed her around,
up and down through the trees,
leading the chorus in the bushes.
The sun set but the singing continued;
our family had expanded,
I put birdseed on the sill,
and opened my window,
the others lead her to me.
We all slept better that night,
knowing Nature had blessed our garden.

6/26/95

Curious Bird

She came through the window,
startling me from a deep sleep.
She flew around and around,
her red feathers flapping furiously,
until she got tired and settled down.
She opened the cage with her beak
and backed herself inside.
I couldn't understand her actions;
months after I had let her free,
she drank some water and ate some seed,
her song rising above my music.
I must admit she pleased me,
locked up in my cage,
the other birds gathered around the window,
peering inside with wild curiosity,
as if they wanted to join her.
I laughed to myself,
such a funny bird I thought,
even my cat found her strange,
giving up the garden for a stuffy room.
After I laughed I cried,
how loved I felt with her
next to me, how beautiful she was.
I never slept better than that night.

6/27/95

Empty Nest

Her babies had flown far away,
the garden was much quieter,
now my cardinal was free to play,
she came to my window,
I opened it and put seed on the inside,
she came in an began to sing.
The sun was just rising,
the sky turned from blue to orange.
I made coffee and lit my pipe,
I just wanted to make her happy.
She picked at my tobacco pouch
and flew back outside to her nest,
the purpose had gone from her flight,
the nest seemed so empty.
As the heat rose, the others gathered
around the birdbath. My cardinal
would have nothing to do with them,
she seemed restless, flying high
above the trees, searching, looking
for anything to amuse her.
Then she flew away, to another garden,
what would bring her back this time?

6/28/95

Back in the Cage

When I awakened,
the birds were singing so loudly,
I tried to go back to sleep but couldn't,
the sky was turning light blue.
It had rained during the night
after a long drought,
it was much cooler outside,
the heat had become intolerable.
The roses and daffodils seemed perkier,
my cardinal came to my window
and pecked forcefully against the glass.
I let her in and watched her
fly furiously around the room,
she perched on her old cage
and sang at the top of her lungs.
She had been gone for days
and now seemed glad to be back,
no wonder the other birds were loud.
I made coffee and lit my pipe,
I opened the cage and let her in,
I left the door of the cage open,
and closed my window.
Now she seemed perfectly happy.

6/29/95

Inside Out

It was the hottest day of the year,
the birds and flowers were wilting.
I turned on my air conditioner,
and kept my window closed.
I put fresh water in the birdbath,
they flocked around it,
splashing and swimming in it.
I watched from a distance
as they enjoyed the summer heat,
I felt lonely and left out
until my cardinal came rapping
and tapping on the glass.
I let her in to enjoy the cool air,
she seemed so lively inside,
flying from chair to table,
bed to dresser, swooping and dipping.
I opened the door of the cage
but she didn't want to go in,
then the others came tapping and rapping,
I decided to let them all in,
they flew around furiously,
ten little birds in one room,
- then the cat walked in!

6/30/95

Bird and Cat

The cat looked at her twice
and yawned, he knew he couldn't
have her, either inside the cage
or out, she flew about the room
in the cool air conditioned air,
she taunted and teased him,
flapping her wings in his face.
He didn't move, but was ready
to pounce, I couldn't stand
the play anymore. I opened
the window and let her out,
he didn't like sharing the room,
didn't like sharing me.
He stretched out with lazy eyes,
I rubbed his stomach and neck,
he was so happy now,
now that she was gone.
I looked out the window
and watched them flutter
in the birdbath, their freedom
unfettered by walls and windows,
graceful in flight, fluttering
in the fresh cool water,
how would they ever become friends?

7/2/95

Love Song

She was singing before all the others,
so early the sun was still asleep.
I stumbled out of bed and made coffee;
it had rained throughout the night.
I lit my pipe and sat back to listen.
Her love song carried across all
the neighboring gardens like the horn
of a lost ship, it was so beautiful.
The others soon joined the chorus.
Then he arrived,
the brightest red feathers I had seen,
his majestic head held high,
his song more shrill than a whistle.
Suddenly, all the others were quiet,
like Miles' trumpet, his song
mesmerized us into a trance.
She could hardly look at him.
Then he lifted his beautiful wings
and flew high above the trees.
No flight was more graceful,
no pattern more interesting.
She heard his call and followed him,
then they were gone;
I never expected to see her again.

7/3/95

Back Again and Again

They were splish-splashing in the birdbath.
I had never seen them so playful.
Then I saw her,
she had returned,
her red feathers brilliant in the sunlight.
But he was not with her,
he had left her perhaps for another.
They were so glad to see her.
I put birdseed on the sill
and left the window wide open.
She took her time,
then flew around the garden
and came over to the window.
She was tired but glad to be home.
She flew around the garden
and came over to the window.
She was tired but glad to be home.
she flew inside and perched
on the stereo where Miles was playing.
"No place like home," she was saying.
She picked some tobacco from my pouch,
and flew vigorously to her old nest.
Her babies had gone,
but she was hoping they would return.
There was no garden like ours,
the waiting had ended.

7/5/95

New Guest

When he flew by,
all their heads turned to look,
his feathers the brightest they had ever seen.
He circled the garden twice
then swooped down and landed.
They were splashing in the birdbath,
she approached cautiously,
not wanting to scare him away.
As she got closer, he stepped back,
so she stopped and waited.
Then suddenly he moved closer.
She panicked and flew up to the maple,
he followed a few branches away.
Then she flew to the roses,
again he followed nearby.
I opened my window
and threw some birdseed outside.
She immediately came to feed,
he followed a few minutes later.
They fed together for a while
until she led him to the birdbath.
They played in the water the rest of the day,
we had a new guest in the garden.

7/12/95

Neglected

He flew away in a fury,
before dawn,
before I had a chance to open my window.
She was angry and I knew why,
I hadn't spread birdseed in days,
had even let the birdbath dry up.
Now I rushed to spread seed,
and put fresh water in the bath.
The other birds were dismayed,
were unhappy she left,
and refused to play in the birdbath.
I didn't know what to do,
I sat in my chair and smoked my pipe,
thinking, wondering, worrying about her.
Now all I could do was wait,
look out the window and wait.
Time stood still,
as if nothing could happen all day.
The others were despondent,
they were waiting as well.
Finally in late evening she returned,
tired and grouchy from the long flight.
She ate some seed by my window,
and flew quickly to her nest.
She had taught me a lesson.

7/14/95

Orange Sun

The heat was intense,
I put cold water in the birdbath,
she had been gone for days,
I had been waiting impatiently
for her return, it was too hot
to smoke but I lit my pipe anyway,
the birds huddled around the bath,
enjoying the cold water.
Then she arrived, tired from the heat,
she immediately dove into the water,
while the others welcomed her home.
I put seed on the windowsill,
but she refused to visit me.
I left the window slightly ajar
and turned on the air conditioning.
Suddenly, all the birds flocked
to the window and slipped inside,
except her. I put a trail of seed
from the outside of the window
to the inside, but she wouldn't
leave the birdbath. I wondered
how long it would be
before she forgave me.

7/14/95

Dew Drop

I sat in the garden
early in the morning;
in the shade of the maple,
amongst the red and white roses,
the birds were singing
and playing in the birdbath.
I was smoking my pipe
and reading a novel of Twain.
My mind flowed down the river
with Huckleberry and Tom,
far away from my peaceful garden,
lost in the world of fiction.
I didn't notice my cardinal
perched calmly above me in the tree.
Suddenly, I felt a drop
hit the top of my head,
I was quickly brought back
to reality, and checked the sky
for rainclouds, then I realized
my bird had dropped off a gift,
I even thought I heard her snickering.
I had to laugh,
and put the book away.

7/17/95

Cat and Bird

The cat looked around twice,
after hearing my cardinal singing,
he was very possessive of his space,
while she flew freely about my room.
She landed lightly next to my pipe
and began picking at my tobacco,
he crouched down and approached slowly,
waiting to pounce.
I watched all this with amusement,
knowing full well he couldn't catch her,
his teeth were bared
and his claws were outstretched.
She pretended to not even see him,
as if he were no danger at all,
which incited him even more.
He crept slowly forward,
waiting patiently until he was close enough,
then he pounced, knocking my pipe
to the floor, and watched
her fly gleefully away out the window
which I had purposefully left open.

7/20/95

Birds and Cat

I couldn't believe it,
the cat was flirting with the birds,
out by the birdbath,
where they were flittering and fluttering,
he had changed his colors,
perhaps knowing how fond of them I was.
I opened the window,
and spread birdseed on the sill, as usual,
then I put the cat's dish of food
out there too, to see what would happen.
Then as I expected, they began to feed
together, as if part of one family,
I found it so charming,
my cardinal was particularly pleased.
She took a bit of cat food in her beak,
and fed it to the cat!
I had never seen anything like it.
Nature could be transformed I figured,
the patterns of flight had altered too,
they flew around the cat
as if he were special,
what a morning I was having!

7/21/95

Never Again

What a nightmare,
she had flown away two weeks before,
I thought for sure she was gone for good.
Then early yesterday she returned,
very tired from the long journey.
I opened my window
and let her in immediately,
she flew around the room
with weary eyes and feathers,
and alighted by my pipe and book.
She picked at my tobacco,
and gently turned the page,
she seemed happy to be back,
and told me she would never leave again.